S0-ACH-924

THE
FATHER'S
PLAN

A BIBLE STUDY FOR DADS

THE
FATHER'S
PLAN

A BIBLE STUDY FOR DADS

ROBERT WOLGEMUTH

THOMAS NELSON
Since 1798

NASHVILLE   DALLAS   MEXICO CITY   RIO DE JANEIRO

© 2010 by Robert D. Wolgemuth

All rights reserved. No portion of this book may be reproduced, stored in a retrieval system, or transmitted in any form or by any means—electronic, mechanical, photocopy, recording, scanning, or other—except for brief quotations in critical reviews or articles, without the prior written permission of the publisher.

Published in Nashville, Tennessee, by Thomas Nelson. Thomas Nelson is a trademark of Thomas Nelson, Inc.

Published in association with the literary agency of Wolgemuth & Associates, Inc.

The publisher is grateful to Steve Halliday of Crown Media, Ltd., for his collaboration and writing skills in developing the content for this book from the text of the *Dad's Bible*; notes written by Robert Wolgemuth.

Thomas Nelson, Inc., titles may be purchased in bulk for educational, business, fund-raising, or sales promotional use. For information, please e-mail SpecialMarkets@ThomasNelson.com.

Unless otherwise noted, Scripture quotations are taken from New Century Version®. © 1987, 1988, 1991, by Thomas Nelson, Inc. Used by permission. All rights reserved.

Scripture quotations marked KJV are from the King James Version of the Bible.

Scripture quotations marked NIV are from the HOLY BIBLE: NEW INTERNATIONAL VERSION®. © 1973, 1978, 1984 by International Bible Society. Used by permission of Zondervan Publishing House. All rights reserved.

Scripture quotations marked NKJV are from THE NEW KING JAMES VERSION. © 1982 by Thomas Nelson, Inc. Used by permission. All rights reserved.

ISBN: 978-1-4185-4305-1

Printed in the United States of America

13 14 [QG] 5 4 3

QG 04-21-15

❖ CONTENTS ❖

♦ INTRODUCTION ♦

WHY STUDY THE BIBLE?

With the busy schedules you and I keep, and with plenty of unfinished tasks clamoring for our attention, is it really necessary to set aside time to study the Bible? Don't we have more productive things to do than spend a few minutes each day with an ancient book? Wouldn't God rather have us use this time to enjoy a second cup of coffee with our wives or hang out with our kids?

These are good questions, for sure. Ones I've asked countless times since getting married and having children.

Let me take a run at an answer that I think makes sense . . .

When I buy something new, I'm always tempted to start assembling without reading the instructions. It's the ultimate challenge. Sure, it looks complicated with all those loose parts littering the floor, but sometimes I whisper to myself, "Am I man enough to put this thing together on my own?"

Unfortunately, more often than not, I've had to go back to those dreaded instructions. Sometimes going it alone has cost me time and energy—and frustration—that I would have avoided had I read the instructions to begin with.

Since you graduated in the top half of your class, you're way ahead of me on this, aren't you?

The Bible is the ultimate instruction Book for your life and mine. It's our inspired source of absolute, divine authority and instruction. The Bible is the most reliable place for you and me to hear God speak. We could dive into managing our lives and trying to assemble the pieces without reading the Instruction Book . . . or we could do the smart thing.

I'm voting for the smart thing.

There is no other book like the Bible. God took more than fifteen hundred years and used forty-five different authors to write it. No small task! You probably know it's the best-selling book of all time, with almost 500 million copies distributed every year and a total of more than 6 *billion* in print. I know it's hard to imagine, but men and women down through the centuries have literally given their lives to preserve the Bible.

Although we could say a lot more about it, the Bible has some very important things to say about itself. Consider just a few:

♦ "[Jesus said to His Father], 'Sanctify them by Your truth. Your word is truth'" (John 17:17 NKJV). **The Bible is truth**.

♦ "Jesus said . . . 'Blessed are those who hear the teaching of God and obey it'" (Luke 11:28). **The Bible brings us blessing**.

♦ "As newborn babies want milk, you should want the pure and simple teaching. By it you can grow up and be saved" (1 Peter 2:2). **The Bible helps us to grow**.

♦ "Your word is like a lamp for my feet and a light for my path" (Psalm 119:105). **The Bible gives us guidance**.

♦ "[The apostle Paul said,] 'I am proud of the Good News, because it is the power God uses to save everyone who believes'" (Romans 1:16). **The Bible gives us power**.

Several years ago, Thomas Nelson Publishers asked me to write the notes to the *Dad's Bible*. It was released in 2007 with the goal of helping men—husbands and fathers—discover for themselves the wonder of this amazing Book. Then the publisher asked me to put together this book, *The Father's Plan: A Bible Study for Dads,* to help you dig for yourself into some of the truth, blessing, growth, guidance, and power found in the Bible. Having your own copy of the *Dad's Bible* would help as you go through this study, but it certainly isn't required. Although you'll find occasional references to stories and comments in the *Dad's Bible,* you'll be able to get by in this study without having one. Your own Bible should work just fine.

My friend Steve Halliday, a gifted editor and writer in his own right, helped me organize this study guide in order to make it both user-friendly and helpful for your study, by yourself or with a group of other men who also want to hear God's voice through the pages of His Word.

We suggest that you block out seven weeks to go through *The Father's Plan*. Maybe this will begin a new habit (they say that it takes forty days to start one) of reading and studying the amazing things God tells us through His Word.

While the arrangement of the contents of each week may vary slightly from lesson to lesson, the material always offers an in-depth opportunity for you to dig into selected Scripture passages and discover the truth that God has for you (we also provide page numbers from the *Dad's Bible* for your convenience). You'll find five separate lessons marked "Day One" through "Day Five" that you should be able to complete in a week. Each day's lesson includes questions that will lead you into a deeper understanding of the text and give you an opportunity to make personal application of God's Word.

Then we encourage you to get together with your group—three to five men who have agreed to do this study together—once a week to discuss what you've been learning. Look for a few "Huddle Up" questions at the end of each week's study to guide your group conversation.

Just so you can see where we're going, take a look at the seven lessons we'll be covering:

1. Your Primary Responsibility as a Father
2. Developing Personal Holiness
3. Building Godly Character into Your Children
4. Asking for Directions
5. Your Closetful of Hats
6. The Greenhouse Effect
7. Pick Me, Pick Me

There's also an epilogue at the end, called "Thou Shalt Smile." This includes some of my favorite funny material. It's tucked back there for no other reason than to give you a chance to smile. You may never get to this material, and that's fine, of course. Or you may use it like the candy dish on the coffee table . . .

popping a sweet in your mouth whenever you walk by. There's no secret reason for this section to be in this study guide. It's there just for fun.

But seriously . . . it's my hope and prayer that *The Father's Plan* study guide inspires you and helps you to begin building a family legacy that lasts . . . for God's glory and for the joy of generations that follow.

Welcome.

Dr. Robert Wolgemuth
Orlando, Florida

YOUR PRIMARY RESPONSIBILITY AS A FATHER

DAY ONE: THE BIG PICTURE

The life setting of the first Old Testament patriarch, Abraham, could not have been more different from ours. He lived thousands of years ago in an agrarian, nomadic, and incredibly low-tech world that looked almost nothing like what we live with every day. He never had to call a customer service person, and his wardrobe consisted essentially of a bathrobe and sandals.

But in one important way, Abraham was *exactly* like you and me: there was nothing in the world he wouldn't have done for his child. He and his wife, Sarah, had waited a long, long time for a son to be born to them, and as Abraham and Sarah's only child, Isaac was the sole heir—and the apple of his daddy's eye.

That's when God stepped up with an awful assignment for this elderly father. God told Abraham to sacrifice his only son—to literally *kill* him. What an incomprehensible request! But because Isaac's dad loved God even more than he loved his only son, Abraham was willing to obey his heavenly Father. He had acted in faith before (when he moved from his homeland to a place he'd never seen), and now he would do it again.

Abraham's willingness to take the life of his son shows that obedience is more important than the potential losses that might result from a sacrifice (see 1 Samuel 15:22, page 293).

The Bible is filled with this principle: If you want to come into God's presence, then everything else—even your most precious possession—has to be offered up to Him. When the Israelites brought an offering from the flock to the altar, it had to be a perfect one. Second best wasn't good enough. If the sacrifice wasn't painful, it wasn't a sacrifice at all. (God was so adamant about this principle that He submitted to it Himself and laid His own unblemished Son on the altar—the cross—in order to give us direct access to Himself. Because of Jesus' death, God looks at you and me through the lens of His Son's righteousness. This is a remarkable thing.)

Abraham is a great example for us. He learned that *God must be first; when I hear His voice, I must obey. Nothing else matters* (page 25). Even though Abraham loved his boy, he was willing to love God even more.

Our children can easily become the center of our lives. This is natural for kid-loving dads . . . but it's not right.

Remember the man named Job? God allowed virtually everything to be taken away from him, including his ten children. Through all the heartbreaking loss, however, Job survived and persevered. The question is, *how?*

Like Abraham, Job feared—that means he held in absolute respect—the almighty God. Throughout the decades that led up to the attack on his home, Job had carefully placed God squarely at the center of his life. The Bible says of Job "He was an honest and innocent man; he honored God and stayed away from evil" (Job 1:1, page 511). Why did he bother to do these right things? Because Job wanted God to be pleased with him so that nothing would get in the way of his relationship with the Lord.

What a difficult but important lesson to learn. While our children are blessings, and we have a significant responsibility to fulfill as their dads, *nothing* is as important as our own relationships with God. In fact, our authority in our families flows out of the example of our submissive relationship with our heavenly Father.

As our authority, God is our Example, our Sustainer, and our Guide. If we want to understand our fatherly responsibilities, we must start by learning who He is and then submit to His leadership—modeling our behavior after His. We cannot become so consumed with our position and our tasks as a dad that we forget we are still children, who need to live under the authority of our Father in heaven . . . and to completely depend on Him.

Leadership is God's responsibility; following is ours. As we learn from His example, our responsibility as dads becomes clear.

OH, AND ONE MORE THING . . .

Although our finite minds cannot completely grasp the idea that Jesus Christ was all of God in human form, the truth is that God literally visited earth in the form of a baby boy. That means that when Jesus walked the earth, He had more authority than anyone who ever left a footprint.

Philippians 2:5–11 (page 1258) tells us that when Jesus lived on earth in the flesh, He was fully God. Although a few times He exercised His authority in full view of everyone (Matthew 21:12, 13, page 1021), at other times He gave up his place and became a servant (Matthew 26:47–54, page 1031).

♦ What could you and I learn as dads from Jesus' example of leading and serving? (See 1 Corinthians 11:1 on page 1222. How would this do for our personal mission statement?)

To Better follow the example of Jesus. Understand I will never be at that level but I should do everything I can to get as close as I can. Live in his image.

DAY TWO: READ ROMANS 13:1–5 (PAGE 1206)

Paul's writing reminds us that, under God and with His blessing, a chain of command exists, a sequence of authorities and subordinates. Depending on the situation, you're either the authority or the subordinate.

From day one we've all been expected to submit to authorities: our parents, a teacher, a coach, a boss, the civil government. This can be especially challenging when we disagree with one of these authorities, but so long as you and I are not being asked to do something that would displease the Lord, we are not given a choice. We're well acquainted with being a subordinate.

But what about the other end of the spectrum? Do you know how to be in authority? If not, you need to learn. Why? Because God has placed you in authority over your home. Of course, you must exercise this authority thoughtfully and fairly, but you do not need to get your child's permission to do so. You have the absolute right and privilege to take responsibility for your family.

How can you and I learn the secrets of being a great superior, a fair judge, a helpful coach? We get our clues by remaining loyal to the authority over us. As we learn what being a faithful subject looks like and what fair leadership feels like, we become better examples to our children—our subordinates—of how they are to act, both inside and outside our homes. Of course, our own example will always speak the loudest.

Listen to this: "Do not be bitter or angry or mad. Never shout angrily or say things to hurt others. Never do anything evil. Be kind and loving to each other, and forgive each other just as God forgave you in Christ" (Ephesians 4:31, 32, page 1253).

Do you see it? The apostle Paul gives us specific instructions and then tells us that our marker of authority and responsibility is what God has done for us through Jesus. It's a great reminder of the balance of leadership and submission.

Authority and responsibility for our families are ours . . . but we must be very careful not to abuse these privileges. We must continue to be faithful subordinates too. It's a great combination.

♦ Some dads are overly strict, taking their authority to levels that offer very little grace. A home such as theirs can feel like a boarding school. And some dads err on the side of passivity by giving their kids too much freedom. (See "Eli, the Passive Father" on page 280.) Their homes are 24/7 recess. Which kind of dad do you tend to be?

> I am the easy one and often the one who prefers to have "fun" instead of teaching.
>
> I would like to be consistant and fair.

♦ How would you describe the "authority" you have been given as a dad? From where does it come? How are you to exercise it? How are you most tempted to abuse it?

> I think the power is just assumed and my wife has done a good job of giving me my place. I struggle with not giving her, her place.

♦ To whom are you accountable for your use of your authority at home? How do you relate to Him? How can your submission to this Authority help you wisely exercise your leadership at home?

> I am accountable to god. I think I love my kids more than anything much like how god loves his children.

♦ How have you seen God work in a positive way through the authority He has given you at home? How has God used both your personal strengths and weaknesses as a father?

The Ability to teach My kids about God is a huge positive. I think using my humor is a positive but my Inability to commit is a Negative

♦ Read Zephaniah 1:2–7 (page 968) and "Walking in Authority" (page 969). You and I have seen football coaches who yell and scream from the sidelines, as well as the "stoics," who barely change their facial expressions, regardless of what's happening on the field. As dads, we have the right to jump up and down and make our demands, and we have the right to hold back. What does "the power of unused power" mean to you? How can you employ this principle in your fathering?

The Power of unused power is just because you have "power" or are given power the true power is IN Not using it just because you have it.

DAY THREE: READ JOSHUA 13:1–7 (PAGE 232)

I love the picture of Joshua, standing over a map of Canaan, awarding real estate to his family—honoring them by declaring it their own land, even though they didn't pay anything for it. I also love the picture of you and me giving our children their own safe place in our homes—physical and emotional territory with their names on it.

As a parent, of course, technically you have the right to go anywhere you choose in your own house. After all, you're the one paying the bills. While you might have the right to push your way into your child's life, however, you don't. Instead, you knock on a closed bedroom door. You ask for permission to enter. And you walk in only when that permission is freely granted. Your love for your children earns you entrance into their "territory." If you try to force your way in, you may pay a dear price.

As the father—the Joshua of your household—you don't lord your authority over your family. Rather, you earn the love and respect of each family member by respecting and loving each one individually . . . giving them the freedom to have their own space and to build their own identity. (See "Insights: Volunteers" on page 251.)

♦ What "physical and emotional territory" have you given to each member of your family? How do you help each of them feel safe in that designated territory?

♦ What generally happens in your home when you try to force your way into your child's life?

♦ How do you try to earn the love and respect of each family member under your roof? What specific things do you do?

♦ In what ways do you show your respect for the members of your family? In what ways do you love each person uniquely? In other words, what does your love and respect look like for every person?

DAY FOUR: READ PSALM 27 (PAGE 561)

Have you ever accepted a task, only to realize later that it was way beyond you? (Of course, you have.) Have you ever landed in a place where the expectations of others overwhelmed you? (Ditto that.) Perhaps it was a project at work that escalated in size, importance, and complexity. Or maybe it was a construction project that quickly took you to places of sheer incompetence. Maybe it's simply the challenge of parenting itself. Or, even though you're an adult—a dad—maybe your parents still hold dreams for you that you can never accomplish.

Like you, I've had many "this-is-bigger-than-me" experiences. And right in the middle of those times, the first verse of Psalm 27 (page 561) washes over me like a cool drink on a hot day: "The Lord is my light and the one who saves me. So why should I fear anyone? The Lord protects my life. So why should I be afraid?"

"That's it," I whisper to myself. "The Lord saves and protects me . . . I have no need to fear." Those moments adjust my perspective. God's promise becomes my hope in the face of total desperation.

♦ What challenges do you face today? How can this promise from Psalm 27 help you in your task as dad? How have you seen God save and protect you already?

♦ In what circumstances at home do you find yourself most likely to fall into the trap of fear? What is it about those situations that makes you afraid? How can embracing King David's claim in Psalm 27 help you overcome those fears?

♦ Look at Deuteronomy 6:4–9 (page 190). Why does Scripture often instruct us to repeat its promises—whether out loud or even in a whisper? What value is there in speaking the words of God's promise?

♦ Look at Isaiah 41:10 (page 740). What does God ask of us, and what does He promise? How will doing these things impact our work as dads?

DAY FIVE: READ 1 PETER 2:4–10 (PAGE 1316)

God calls every Christ-following dad to be a "holy priest." So what does that mean? (Read "Walking in Authority" on page 1315.)

We are to know His Word and listen to His voice so we can say to our families, "This is what God is saying to us." God calls you and me to instruct and encourage His people in our homes and to share His blessings with them.

We stand in the presence of a holy God to plead our families' case. And we must begin our prayers by confessing our own inadequacy and sin.

You're a card-carrying priest. Your family is your congregation, and your home is your sanctuary. This priesthood might not be the occupation that helps you pay the bills, but it may well be the most important thing you ever do.

♦ You may not have "Rev." in front of your name, but you're a priest. What does it mean to you that God has called you to be His "priest" in your home? How seriously have you taken this calling?

♦ What does it mean to "listen" to God's voice? How much time do you normally spend each week in God's Word and in prayer by yourself?

♦ What do you believe God is saying to you as your family's priest *right now*? What do think He's saying to your wife and kids? How do you plan to communicate this message to your family?

♦ Describe the sort of praying you do for your family in a typical week. How much time do you spend praying for each member of your household? Would it be a good idea to invest more time? Why?

♦ Why is it important in your calling as a priest to begin by confessing your own inadequacy and sin? How can this practice free you rather than burden you?

HUDDLE UP: FOR GROUP DISCUSSION

Look back over your notes from this past week and share one or two things that were especially significant to you.

The following questions will help your group to review:

♦ When you and I read the stories of Abraham trusting God—moving to a place he didn't know, being asked to sacrifice his son—we know what's going to happen. We have the whole account recorded in our Bibles, so there's no suspense for us. But what would it have been like to be Abraham? When in your past has God asked you to trust Him? Where is God asking you to trust Him right now?

♦ You and I live under authority. How do we treat our superiors? Do our kids hear us criticizing those whom God has placed in authority over us? (Politicians who are not from our favorite party? Policemen hiding with their radar guns fixed on us?) Is it possible that our children will be tempted to think of their dads in the same way we think of those in authority over us? (Ouch.) What should we do about this?

◆ As dads, do we have the right to walk into our kid's room unannounced? What would Joshua say about a family's right to their own space?

◆ Have you ever wished that you could turn in your "Dad Badge"? This is more work than you bargained for. What can you do about this?

◆ You're a priest in your home. You really are. What does this mean for Mrs. Priest? For your little parishioners?

DADS IN THE BIBLE

The New Testament tells a wonderful story about a responsible (and passionate) father, a Jewish leader named Jairus. On page 1043 you can read how his indomitable spirit and courage led to healing for his little girl. Amazing.

A CLOSING PRAYER

Have someone in your group ask each man, "How can we pray for you this week?" It's a good idea for each dad to write down these requests so he can remember them for his own daily time of prayer. Then someone can volunteer to close this time with a spontaneous prayer.

Or here's a prayer someone can read aloud:

Dear Father in heaven, we love You. Thank You for our families. And thank You for giving us the responsibility to be leaders in our homes. Thank You for Jesus' example of strength and humility. Help us to accept our important role as priests with our families. We want to please You in everything we say and do. Thank You for Your Holy Spirit, who gives us wisdom. We are very grateful. Amen.

DEVELOPING PERSONAL HOLINESS

DAY ONE: THE BIG PICTURE

Many years ago, a very silly television ad featured two grown-ups arguing over one of the more critical and controversial issues in the news: Is Certs a breath mint or a candy mint? You (or your dad) may remember the surprising conclusion: Certs was both.

The Christian tradition I grew up in called itself—and still does—the "holiness movement." As a young boy, I became very aware of people's conduct. I noticed when folks used expletives in normal conversation, drank excessively, gambled, or went to movies that celebrated immoral behavior. The frequent Bible verse used in sermons and Sunday school lessons for young and old was Leviticus 20:7 (page 131): "Sanctify yourselves therefore, and be ye holy, for I am the LORD your God" (KJV).

Inarguable evidence that holiness is important to God.

Then, as a young adult, I was exposed to another kind of tradition with a very different flavor. This one clearly was grace-based. "There's nothing," I was told, "that you can do to earn God's pleasure." No conduct—even if people cleaned up their acts and stopped doing the foolish and harmful things listed above—is good enough to save them from God's judgment. The verse used to make this point was Isaiah 64:6 (page 766): "But we are all as an unclean thing, and all our righteousnesses are as filthy rags" (KJV). Or Ephesians 2:8, 9 (page 1250): "You have been saved by grace through believing.

You did not save yourselves; it was a gift from God. It was not the result of your own efforts, so you cannot brag about it."

Inarguable evidence that grace is our only hope.

This week we're going to talk about holiness. And we're going to look at holiness through the lens of grace. Why? Because, just as Certs is both a candy *and* a breath mint, your walk with Christ, and mine, clearly includes both holiness *and* grace.

When our children were small, sometimes at dinner my wife and I would suggest that we use "White House manners." We'd then pretend that we were sitting down at a state dinner. The secret to good manners was envisioning a setting where we were in the presence of very important people.

The secret to living a holy life is remembering in whose presence you and I are living. The prophet Isaiah surely had an overwhelming sense of God's Spirit; his experience profoundly impacted how he saw himself. (See "Godly Character" on page 702.) What's also interesting is that my conduct affects my character, which affects my conduct, which affects my character. Good conduct that comes from good character is not playacting. There's nothing phony about it. Back to the Certs ad for just one more painful moment: like the breath and candy mint, character and conduct are inseparable.

OH, AND ONE MORE THING . . .

As a dad with small children, I often discussed this issue with my wife. "Let's make sure that our children catch a glimpse of what it might be like to actually be in the same room as the Creator of the universe." This may sound a little simplistic . . . to have your conduct—your ability to live a holy life—affected simply by your close proximity to God. But it's absolutely true. Just ask Isaiah (read the first five verses of Isaiah 6 on page 701).

♦ How would you conduct yourself differently today if Jesus Christ accompanied you both physically and visibly everywhere you went?

DAY TWO: READ ACTS 2:26–41 (PAGE 1152)

As important as it is to understand that my efforts toward holiness (good conduct) are required but that God's grace (His forgiveness when I mess up) is what cleans the slate, it's even more imperative to understand that the Christian life really isn't about either of these.

It's about Jesus, His atonement (what He accomplished on the cross), and His *choice* to save you and me, or as He said to a man named Nicodemus late one night, the gift of being "born again" (See John 3, page 1116). The gift of salvation.

No words can adequately describe the face of a child when she realizes that something she's really wanted . . . is finally hers. That moment when you say, "It's for you," is an awesome thing.

The author of the book of Acts, taking a cue from Jesus' late-night conversation with Nicodemus, records the time when the apostle Peter preached the sermon of his life (Acts 2, page 1152). Jesus had just returned to heaven and had passed the leadership mantle to His disciples. Like a brother who just sent off his older sibling to college, Peter stepped up to the plate. Looking at the huge crowd before him, Peter spoke these words about a very special present: "Receive the gift of the Holy Spirit . . . for you [and] for your children" (vv. 38, 39). In effect, Peter was saying, "It's for you, my friends. This gift is for you."

That day, three thousand people received the gift of salvation and the filling of the Holy Spirit. None of them would ever forget that moment.

When did you receive the gift of salvation? And how many of your friends and colleagues need to hear the words, "It's for you, my friend. It's for you"? God's Holy Spirit is the perfect present for you, for your children, and for everyone on your list.

◆ When did you place your faith in Jesus Christ? What led up to your decision? What has flowed out of your decision?

◆ Who among your family, friends, and colleagues need to hear the good news about eternal life in Christ? List a few of them. What keeps you from praying that God would open a door to salvation for every person you listed?

◆ What is the best thing you have experienced so far since receiving God's gift of salvation? What has been the most surprising thing?

♦ How do you plan to share the good news (the gospel) with your children? What resources will you use? What plan do you have in place for their spiritual growth once they ask Jesus Christ to become the Lord of their lives?

DAY THREE: READ 1 THESSALONIANS 4:3 (PAGE 1271)

Paul did not direct the recipients of this courageous letter to "stay away from sexual sins" because God is some cosmic spoilsport, straight out of Victorian England. He told these men to live this way because if they didn't, their careless disobedience would shatter their hearts.

When sexual sin of any description tempts you, immediately think of your family. If you succumb to temptation, they may not feel the effects right away, but sooner or later, they will (and more likely, sooner). The impact of impurity rarely remains private, and it's never harmless, not even when the involved parties give their mutual consent. Sexual sin causes families staggering amounts of grief and untold anguish. And it's a sin not only against your wife and kids, but against God Himself (see Genesis 39:9, page 48).

When you model sexual purity for your family, your children benefit from the strong example you provide. Your own discipline also helps guard them as they grow.

Sexual purity is not God's great practical joke on men whose veins course with testosterone. Purity is His blessing. It's His promise. If you cross this

31

line, you and your family will suffer the severe consequences. So please don't cross it.

♦ Why does sexual sin tend to have such serious consequences? Take some time to mentally walk through the Bible. Whose lives portrayed there were torn and shattered by sexual sin? What consequences did these people have to endure?

♦ Try an uncomfortable thought experiment. Attempt to imagine, in detail, what might happen to your own family following some sexual transgression on your part. What happens to your marriage? Your kids? Your reputation? Your home? Your church relationships? Your Christian witness at work? Your ability to relax and sleep?

♦ Who do you know personally that has suffered the consequences of some sexual sin? What happened? Who was hurt? How has it affected that person's future?

♦ In what situations do you feel most vulnerable to sexual temptation? What can you do now to prepare for those situations? To whom can you be accountable for your sexual purity?

♦ How often do you think about God's holiness? What does it mean to you? Why do you think the Bible says that no one who lacks personal holiness will see God (see Hebrews 12:14, page 1304)?

DAY FOUR: READ JEREMIAH 50:1–5 (PAGE 831)

Jeremiah had to be one of history's most disciplined "prayer warriors." This man regularly stayed in touch with God. Most of his writing includes the words "This is what the Lord says." Jeremiah had such an intimate and regular walk with God that he had no trouble repeating the words he had heard from heaven.

Can you conceive of a higher goal than to have this kind of connection with the sovereign Creator of the cosmos? Can you imagine the thrill of being led every day by His almighty hand? If this sounds good to you, then give it a shot. Make contact with your heavenly Father a part of your daily routine. Getting up a few minutes early each day—before diving into your morning—to spend time alone with Him is a good place to start.

You might be able to do this simply by deciding to do it. If so, that's great. Those of us who lack such strong discipline, however, might need a daily reminder to spend time in prayer. Asking someone to hold us accountable for a regular prayer time, or finding someone to pray with us once in a while (your wife can be a terrific prayer partner), will help to build consistency.

As you talk with the Lord, don't forget to listen. Listen for His lead. Our goal is to achieve the kind of deep intimacy that Jeremiah enjoyed.

♦ How would you describe your current prayer life? How satisfied are you with the way things are? What would it take for you to make some improvements?

♦ Describe some of your best experiences in prayer. What did you pray for? How did God respond? How can you leverage these high points to deepen your prayer life?

♦ What does it mean to "listen" to God in prayer? How has He spoken to you through prayer in the past? How do you recognize His voice? How do you know it's not the voice of an impostor?

♦ Who do you know that you might call a modern-day "prayer warrior"? What drives this person to prayer? What kind of track record in prayer does he have? How can you benefit from this person's experiences in prayer? What keeps you from asking him to become your prayer "mentor"?

DAY FIVE: READ ROMANS 5:1–8 (PAGE 1195)

All of us suffer. This may include our own physical pain, the loss of a job, or walking through agonizing struggles with a family member or a close friend. Suffering is a fact of life, but Paul gives us good news: suffering can lead to perseverance.

Perseverance keeps us from quitting and helps us hang in there when we don't feel like it, when discouragement and frustration make us want to give up. And perseverance leads to godly character that your children will clearly see. Character includes many nonnegotiables: truth-telling, faith, fidelity, kindness, transparency, tenderness . . . and holiness. We build all of these traits through perseverance, which suffering perfects. And in the end, character leads to hope.

Because of hope we can look forward to today . . . and tomorrow . . . and next week. God is at work, fashioning us to be his men. God gives us a future, and then He plants hope in our hearts to trust in His presence until we eventually get to where He wants us to be.

♦ How can suffering lead to perseverance? In what ways has it led to perseverance in your own life? How have you responded to suffering in ways that have *not* led to greater perseverance?

♦ In what arenas of life do you most feel like quitting? What responsibilities as a father make you want to give up? What can keep you going when you really want to just cash it all in?

♦ What kind of hope keeps you going when times get tough? What do you consider your fondest hope? On what is this hope built? How does this hope differ from mere wishful thinking?

♦ What kind of future has God set before you? How is He building you into "His man"? How does suffering fit in to this scenario? Where does perseverance fit? How about character? Where does hope fit in? How do all of these things help you to become more holy?

Huddle Up: For Group Discussion

Look back over your notes from this past week, and share one or two things that felt especially significant to you.

The following questions will help your group to review:

♦ What pictures come to mind when you think of someone being called "holy"? What part does God's grace play in the development of your own personal holiness? Why are character and conduct inseparable? What happens in your life as you begin to think of God's actual presence with you at every moment of every day?

♦ What is the best gift that God ever gave you? How has this gift shaped your life? Why does the apostle Peter call the Holy Spirit a "gift"? What does it mean to be "born again"? How are you sharing the good news with others? How are you sharing it with your own family?

♦ Why do you think the Bible spends so much time warning believers against sexual sin? How have you seen sexual sin devastate the lives of others? Why would Joseph call sexual sin a sin against God? (See Genesis 39:9, page 48.) What does the warning of Hebrews 12:14 (page 1304) mean to you?

♦ In prayer we connect with God in a way that increasingly brings us into closer alignment with His will and His desires. How would you describe your prayer life? What are its strengths and weaknesses? How do you "listen" to God in prayer? How are you modeling effective prayer for your family members?

♦ How are personal holiness and perseverance related? How can you help one another to persevere in your faith? How does perseverance lead to both a bright future and a glorious hope? What makes it hard for you to persevere?

DADS IN THE BIBLE

In the prayer recorded in Psalm 25, King David gives us a picture of the kind of man who deeply wants to be the person he knows the Lord God wants him to be—a man who understands and embodies personal holiness. Read about this on page 560.

A CLOSING PRAYER

Have someone in your group ask each man, "How can we pray for you this week?" Again, it's a good idea for everyone to write down these requests so that each father can remember them in his own daily time of prayer. You could end your time together by seeing if a volunteer would be willing to offer a spontaneous prayer. Or someone could read aloud the following prayer:

Dear Father in heaven, thank You for the Gift of the Holy Spirit, who daily works in our lives to make us more like Christ. We praise you for giving to us, through faith, the very righteousness of Jesus. We ask that this week You might help each of us to grow in personal holiness as we seek to listen to Your voice and remember that, even though we do not see You, You are with us at every moment of every day, wherever we go. We are amazed . . . and thankful. Amen.

◆ NOTES ◆

3

BUILDING GODLY CHARACTER INTO YOUR CHILDREN

DAY ONE: THE BIG PICTURE

Last week we double-clicked on the whole idea of conduct and character . . . for yourself. This week we're going to look at how to transfer this idea to our children.

The three biblical heroes of "fiery furnace" fame lived centuries before Paul wrote the words of Romans 5:4 (page 1197), but they make terrific poster boys for the apostle's main point. Paul wrote, "We also rejoice in our sufferings, because we know that suffering produces perseverance; perseverance, character; and character, hope" (NIV).

You may remember from Sunday school or reading a kid's Bible storybook the celebrated account from Daniel 3. In an attempt to bring unity to his kingdom, Babylon's king Nebuchadnezzar created a one-size-fits-all god—a huge idol made of gold. He fully expected everyone, including the Israelites whom he had captured, to bow down to it. Somehow, the king misjudged the godly character of three young men named Shadrach, Meshach, and Abednego.

This trio of God-fearing believers did not hesitate to stand up to the crushing pressure of the pagan culture surrounding them. They refused to bow down. Enraged, Nebuchadnezzar sentenced them to die and tossed them into a furnace. It may have been the same furnace he had used to refine the gold for his idol. Looks like these men were refined before they hit the flames. As you probably remember, God sent an angel to join the young men standing in the flames, sparing their lives.

You and I can read about Daniel and these three young men in Daniel 1 and 2 (starting on page 898). We see that even though these men were far from home, in a place of incredible external pressures to disobey their God—like a business trip that lasted for years—their internal convictions trumped everything that tempted them.

We can rightly assume that since these young men were Jews, most of what they had learned about God and living in obedience to Him, they learned at home.

OH, AND ONE MORE THING . . .

Godly character doesn't "just happen." It grows best in children when their father teaches it . . . and models it. Jewish dads were famous for this. When kids see their dad standing up for what he believes, their own character begins to take root. When they witness how God's love and grace affect his thinking, his lifestyle, and his decisions, it blossoms in them. Sure, a commitment to godly living can sometimes land believers in a pretty hot place—but God has plenty of angels to dispatch. He even has a few who are particularly skilled at protecting his obedient children from the flames.

♦ If your children suddenly were to be taken from you and brought to a pagan nation far away, how do you think they would fare spiritually? What have they learned about godly character from your example?

DAY TWO: READ 1 SAMUEL 16:1–7 (PAGE 293)

Scripture describes King Saul as tall and handsome. He stood out in a crowd. In our day, he would've been a sure candidate for *People* magazine's 100 Most Beautiful People. But Saul did not wow God. In fact, a few years into Saul's reign, God rejected him as king. Saul's imposing exterior did not impress the Almighty, because the king's character had become completely corrupt.

So God eventually instructed Samuel to find another king, telling the prophet to look on the inside at the character of the man, and not at his photogenic appearance.

Think for a second about how much effort we exert on our outsides. We try to eat right and exercise. We carefully groom ourselves and collect enough clothes to fill our closets. All good things…but to God, we're completely transparent. He looks directly into who we really are—our thoughts, our motives, our desires . . . our hearts.

It's the same for our kids. In a culture mesmerized by exterior appearance, it's critical for you and me to remind our children that God cares much more about their interior, their personal character.

This does not mean we should ignore our bodies. They are, after all, the temples where God's Spirit lives (see 1 Corinthians 6:19, page 1218). But while Paul saw real value in physical training, he also insisted that "godliness has value for all things, holding promise for both the present life and the life to come" (1 Timothy 4:8 NIV, page 1280). The challenge is to pay more attention to who we are than to what we look like.

♦ Why do you think Saul's character had become "completely corrupt"? He started out well; what changed? What led to his downfall? (See 1 Samuel 10:22, page 287; 12:20, page 289; 13:7, page 289; 15:24, page 293; 18:12, 15, 29, page 297; 28:20, page 307.) What can you learn from Saul's collapse?

♦ How much time per day do you spend getting your "outside" in order? How much time per day do you spend getting your "inside" in order? Are you satisfied with this comparison?

♦ How have you addressed issues of character with your children? How have they responded? How effective do you think your efforts have been so far at building character into your children?

♦ What sort of "character building" exercises could your whole family try? As you look at each member of your family (yourself included), what specific character issues do you think need to be addressed?

DAY THREE: READ ROMANS 12:1–2 (PAGE 1205)

In these verses, Paul was saying, "Don't let the world suck you into its mold." What a powerful word picture of what it's like to live in our culture! Think about how easily we can become something that we had no intention of becoming, almost without effort. It reminds me of hot, molten plastic getting sucked into a mold.

So what's a man to do? Thankfully, Paul helps us out. He challenges us to avoid being pressed into a cultural mold that would transform us into something ungodly. Instead, he wants us to "be changed within" (v. 2), allowing God to shape the raw material of our lives into His image.

And how do we go through such a spiritual metamorphosis? Again, Paul tells us directly: "Do not be shaped by this world; instead be changed within by a new way of thinking." What we read, what we log on to, what we channel surf to, what we listen to, who we follow as heroes. . . all of these influences mold our minds through the ideas and attitudes that hide in the crevices.

The same principle, of course, holds true for our children. Their character will be shaped from outside pressure or it will be transformed from the inside. God calls us to partner with Him on this inner transformation, first in our own thinking, and then in our children's. Neither you nor I, of course, can accomplish such a feat through sheer willpower alone. The Holy Spirit, working in our hearts, must bring about this transformation (see Galatians 5:19–25, page 1247).

We don't need to fear the world's mold. But we must be very careful to remain vigilant. Our children's godly character is at stake, and the stakes get no higher than that.

◆ How does our culture try to suck you into its mold? In what areas are you most at risk? What strategies do you have in place to counteract these effects?

♦ How does our culture try to suck your children into its mold? In what areas are they most at risk? What strategies do you have in place to counteract these effects?

♦ What "new way of thinking" did Paul have in mind? How does it come about? How can you cooperate with God to bring about your own personal transformation? What can you do as a dad to help this transformation take place in your children?

♦ Take some time to linger on Philippians 4:8 (page 1261). What sorts of things did Paul tell us to think about? How can you help your children think about such things?

DAY FOUR: READ PROVERBS 1:8–19 (PAGE 635)

Dad, you are smarter and wiser than your children. You have experienced more of life, and you see things they cannot. So, how can this wisdom be transferred to the next generation? What can your kids do to receive it? An important word in Proverbs 1 says it all. That word is *listen.*

Your children must learn how to listen to you . . . with their ears *and* their eyes. If your children are not watching you, not looking at you as you speak with them, then they're not listening. And if your children are not listening, then your experience and wisdom will do them no good.

Some of this, of course, depends on how you speak with your child. If you aren't intentional about spending one-on-one, face-to-face time with your children, then they may *never* listen to you. If your conversations with them always occur on the run or in a crowded room, then they will never pick them up. (My wife says, "You can't parent from the back of your head.")

"My child, listen to your father's teaching and do not forget your mother's advice" (v. 8). Can you imagine Solomon saying such a thing to his son as the boy's eyes were texting on his iPhone or while Solomon continued reading his newspaper? No. Such a statement has power only when the father looks straight into his child's eyes. If you want your children to listen with both their ears and their eyes, you must do the same.

You *are* smarter than your kids. You *do* have much wisdom to share. Take confidence in this truth. Then find ways to communicate your wisdom intentionally, lovingly, in a normal tone of voice, without distractions, and with plenty of eye contact. This is the way godly character begins to take root in the fertile soil of your child's life.

♦ What wisdom do you have to pass along to your children? In what areas would you consider yourself "wise"? In what areas do you consider yourself not so wise? How can you best tap into your strengths and compensate for your weaknesses?

♦ How successfully did your dad model character for you? How well do you model for your children the art of listening with your ears and your eyes? How do you keep yourself from getting distracted when your children try to speak with you? If someone were to ask your children, "Does your dad *really* listen to you?" what do you think they'd say?

♦ What ways have you found to communicate your wisdom: (a) intentionally; (b) lovingly; (c) in a normal tone of voice; (d) without distractions; and (e) with plenty of eye contact?

♦ What character traits do you hope your children acquire from modeling their behavior after you? What character traits do they have that you wish you did? How can you help each other grow in godliness?

DAY FIVE: READ JAMES 2:14–26 (PAGE 1309)

Show-and-tell isn't just a game for kids at school. It's a great picture of our walk with God and a wonderful formula for building godly character into our kids.

James discussed the delicate balance between faith (tell) and works (show) in relation to our salvation. Of course, we don't gain entrance to the Holy One by being good enough. Only our simple confession of repentance and faith in the crucified and risen Jesus Christ will give us the full measure of His grace.

But there are some who distort this truth, who declare that faith by itself is good enough. James calls such a faith "dead" (vv. 17, 26). "What good is it, my brothers," he asked, "if a man claims to have faith but has no deeds?" (v. 14).

If you say that you believe in Jesus, then you'd better be ready to back up your claim with action. And if we're going to successfully pass along our faith to our family members, then we must back up our profession of faith with good deeds. We all know some dads who are good talkers. They openly speak about how much they love God and others. But their words are thoroughly vacant unless their actions support them. We're certainly not going to fool our families! If you want your children to develop godly character, then you must show them what it looks like. At home.

James has the formula. Work *and* faith . . . do *and* believe . . . obey *and* trust . . . show *and* tell. (Remember week two . . . holiness *and* grace.)

♦ How would you describe, in your own words, the "delicate balance" between faith and works in relation to our salvation?

♦ How much "dead" faith do you see around you?

♦ How do you demonstrate to your family that what you *say* you believe you *actually* believe?

♦ Would you be happy if your children mirrored the character qualities you regularly display?

HUDDLE UP: FOR GROUP DISCUSSION

Look back over your notes from this past week, and share one or two things that felt especially significant to you.

The following questions will help your group to review:

♦ What can you probably assume about the home life of the three Hebrew young men who got tossed into the furnace because of their faith? Based on their response to the king, what lessons do you think were emphasized in their homes? What "hot places" might await your own children? What can you do now to prepare them for these?

♦ From what you know about Saul, do you think he'd win a wide audience if he lived in our day? What does it mean to look "inside" a person? How is this possible? How can you best teach your children to balance taking care of their "outsides" with taking care of their "insides"? What are you modeling in this regard?

◆ How does the world try to suck you into its mold? How does it try to suck your children into its mold? What do you and your children spend a significant amount of time reading, logging on to, channel surfing to, listening to, and following? In what way does a transformed life begin with a transformed mind? What process is involved in transforming one's mind?

◆ How well do you believe your children *really* listen to you? How can you teach them to listen to you both with their ears *and* with their eyes? How much "face time" do you give your kids? How much one-on-one time do you schedule for each child? How intentional and loving are your interactions with your children?

◆ What is the necessary connection between faith and works? How does what you believe show up in what you do? How can you better *show* and *tell* others about your relationship with Christ?

DADS IN THE BIBLE

The Bible gives many examples of fathers who were anything but character-builders for their kids. But the Scriptures overflow with illustrations that show how our heavenly Father offers us a perfect example. Read about this on page 316.

A CLOSING PRAYER

Have someone in your group ask each man, "How can we pray for you this week?" Remember that it's a good idea for each participant to write down these requests; that makes it easier for everyone to remember them in their own daily times of prayer. Close your time by asking a volunteer to offer a spontaneous prayer. Or someone could read aloud the following suggested prayer:

Dear Father in heaven, You are so amazingly good to us. Day after day and week after week, You shower us with Your blessings, all of which flow out of Your excellent character. Father, help us to mirror Your example. Teach us and encourage us to help our children develop into young men and women who love You and who long to please You in everything they do. We praise You for who You are to us. Amen.

4

ASKING FOR DIRECTIONS

DAY ONE: THE BIG PICTURE

The Global Positioning System (GPS) has changed everything, and not just in cars. In fact, many cell phones and other hand-held devices also feature applications of this technological wonder. What GPS has changed is the frequent citation of the tired adage about men never stopping to ask for directions. We don't *need* to stop and ask for directions anymore, because that nice lady's voice reassuringly emanating from the GPS means our wives no longer feel compelled to ask us to *please* stop and ask directions because we've passed the same 7-Eleven three times. No, now the GPS confidently tells me: "Right turn in 1.6 miles," or my personal favorite, "Recalculating . . . look for an opportunity to make a U-turn."

Okay, so you and I don't need to stop and ask for directions, because we have these terrific devices. It's all good.

Still, I would like to make a couple of observations. See if you can identify with these: (1) Since my faithful GPS informs me about every twist and turn I need to take until I safely reach my destination, I have stopped learning how to get from point A to point B in unfamiliar cities. I used to unfold old-fashioned maps the width of a queen-size bedsheet and actually learn the layout of the city. No more. This means that on the rare occasions when the GPS fails me, I find myself in very deep weeds. And (2) I still have a hard time asking for directions. And, frankly, not only directions, but help in general, even when I know I'm in trouble.

In a high-pitched battle with the Amalekites, even Moses discovered that he needed help (the story starts at Exodus 17:8, page 83). Standing on a high ridge overlooking the battlefield, Moses was able to watch his forces fight the enemy. We don't know where Moses got this idea, but he discovered that when he held his hands high, the Israelite army prevailed. But when his arms grew tired and fell to his side, his army lost ground. So, Moses' two lieutenants, Aaron and Hur, stood next to their leader and held his hands high for him. As a result, the Israelites triumphed. What a spectacular picture!

The man charged with being the leader of his people gave his "family" a victory by asking his friends to help. We have no indication that Moses found this hard to do. We don't know if he had to swallow his pride and admit that his arms grew too heavy to hold up by himself. We know only that he got the help he needed . . . and doing this saved his nation, his family.

God never intended for you and me to do our jobs as dads by ourselves; that's why He has surrounded us with faithful people. We're married and have wives to help us. We also have pastors (for us), youth ministers (for our kids), extended family, neighbors, coaches, teachers, close friends . . . able supporters in the daunting task of effective fathering. Use them. You cannot be an effective dad all by yourself. In fact, you aren't even supposed to try.

Oh, and One More Thing . . .

Years ago, when we lived in Tennessee, I used to pass the high school football practice field on my drive home from work. Some clever carpenter-dad had built a sturdy wooden tower for the coach and his assistants. It was probably ten feet high, tall enough to give the coaches exactly what they needed to see their young athletes executing the new plays for the big game that weekend. The tower gave them perspective.

Now that we have GPS, you and I are in danger of reaching our destination safely—but failing to understand how the city is laid out. We get there, but we don't really know *how*. If you were to build a tower above your family, you could look down on how they—and you—are doing.

♦ Who are the assistant coaches you should invite to stand on the structure with you? In what area of your life do you find it most challenging to ask for directions?

DAY TWO: READ EXODUS 32:19–25 (PAGE 100)

Prior to taking a business trip to visit with God atop a smoking mountain, Moses left Aaron in charge of the nation of Israel. With the leader gone, the Israelites saw an opportunity for some good, old-fashioned complaining. They whined and asked Aaron to make them new gods because they had grown tired of worshipping a God they could not see.

Aaron quickly caved in to the pressure and let the people build an idol—a human-made, make-believe god. The out-of-control Israelite family soon became comic relief for the surrounding nations. Israel's enemies laughed at them—and the sad entertainment resulted directly from Aaron's atrocious leadership. "How funny it is," these other nations must have said, "to see a family in which the children make the rules."

Be the dad in your house. Despite the temptation to let your family's complaining and whining win out over your solid leadership, don't let your home become one where children make the rules. Let the entertainment under your roof come from God-honoring fun, and give mockers no material to tickle their scornful funny bones.

♦ What kind of pressures led Aaron to cave in to the Israelites' illegitimate demands? How could he have resisted these pressures? How does Aaron's situation parallel what goes on in many homes today? In what way do some parents today let their children make the rules for their households?

♦ How do you deal with your children's complaining and whining? What strategies do you have in place? What has worked? What hasn't?

♦ How would you characterize your leadership in the home? What are your top five "rules"? How do you communicate them to your children? How do your children respond to your leadership? What are your strengths and weaknesses as your family's leader?

DAY THREE: READ ECCLESIASTES 4:9-12 (PAGE 678)

Families are a lot of work. There's always something to pick up around the house . . . something to clean up, fix up, or put up. And most of us—especially dads—would rather be served than serve. Although we wouldn't call it laziness, between you and me, this is pretty much what it is.

In Ecclesiastes 4:9–12, King Solomon delivers a timely message. He's telling us to pitch in. He's challenging us to change a diaper, empty the dishwasher, or pull out the vacuum cleaner. He's reminding us that this family thing requires a team effort; we work together for one another. Helping out is one simple way of showing our families that we are thankful for them. As Solomon's examples point out, we're all better off when we help each other. As a matter of fact, the strength of a family often depends on individual members pitching in wherever they see a need.

Look around. You have plenty of little things to do. Rally the troops and get busy. Lead the charge with your example. If you want help from *them* when you need it, then begin by offering *your* help when they need it.

♦ Be honest: would you rather be served at home than serve? If so, how can you overcome this tendency? What does Matthew 20:26–28 (page 1020) say to you about this?

♦ What does it mean to you to "pitch in" around the house? Give several examples of how you help family members get jobs done.

♦ How do you show your family that you're thankful for them?

♦ What "little things" around your house need to get done that haven't been getting done? How can you help? What specifically can you do to "rally the troops" and accomplish these neglected tasks?

DAY FOUR: READ 1 SAMUEL 12:23 (PAGE 289)

Shortly before he died, my dad admitted that he lacked the strength to do anything but pray for his children. I told him that praying for us was a mighty gift, one without equal.

It's easy to take prayer lightly. Sometimes we forget what an incredible privilege it is; we forget that petitioning the Almighty is an amazing thing.

Dads must take prayer seriously. It's one of the most important things we can do to serve our families.

Thank the Lord for His goodness, let Him know your concerns for your family, confess your own weaknesses, and ask Him for the help you need. If you want to succeed as a dad, you must admit that the assignment is bigger than you are—and when you pray, you not only admit your inadequacy, but you connect to the One who is far bigger than your assignment

♦ What does your personal practice say to your household about your beliefs regarding prayer? By looking at your example, would they say you believe prayer is "a gift without equal"?

♦ In what ways is prayer "an amazing thing"? What's so amazing about it?

♦ Where would you rank prayer among the most important things you do as a dad? What place does it have on your schedule?

♦ Many people use the acronym ACTS to remind them of the four key elements of prayer: *adoration—being in God's presence and being filled with awe; confession—leveling with God about specifics in your life; thanksgiving—going over the list of gifts God has lavished on you;, and supplication—your list of concerns, needs, and requests.* In which of these is your prayer life strong? In which is it weak? What are you willing to do to improve your prayer life, especially concerning your family?

DAY FIVE: READ 1 SAMUEL 1:21–28 (PAGE 277)

For centuries, Christian parents have brought their children to church for a special ceremony in which the parents publicly acknowledge their little person as a blessing . . . a gift on loan from God. And they publicly promise to bring him or her up in the Christian faith. This takes place in front of men and women they know, people who love them enough to remind them of this promise—family and friends who would dare to challenge them if they ever saw the couple begin to drift from this pledge.

Hannah brought Samuel to the temple as a small child. We don't know if her husband, Elkanah, accompanied her, but if he did, he had a part in this promise. In any case, Hannah's vow to "give [Samuel] back to the Lord" (v. 28) provides a tremendous model for us and our children.

When you bring your child to the front of your church and present him or her to the Lord, you are promising to be a godly example for this child. You are asking your minister, your family, and your friends to do the same. And you're putting the world on notice. "I'm going to be a Christian father," you say. "To succeed, I need some help from you . . . and I expect us to hold each other accountable on this one."

♦ In what ways do you consider children a blessing? How are they gifts on loan from God?

♦ Have you had your children dedicated (baptized, christened, etc.) in church? If so, what sort of promise did you make publicly to bring them up in the Christian faith? (If not, you should schedule this soon.) How have you followed through on this promise?

♦ How have you asked friends and family to support you and challenge you in your attempts to raise your children in the faith? In what ways could you use their help?

♦ How is Hannah's vow to give her son back to the Lord an example for you? What does this story say to you about your own children and their connection to God and to the church?

Huddle Up: For Group Discussion

Look back over your notes from this past week, and share one or two things that seemed especially significant to you.

The following questions will help your group to review:

♦ How hard is it for you to ask for directions? What experience have you had with GPS? Who are the faithful partners God has placed around you to assist you with directions in your role as dad? What kind of "tower" are you constructing to help you get an accurate perspective regarding your family's development?

♦ What part did the complaining and whining of the children of Israel play in Aaron's caving in to their ungodly demands? How do you tend to react to your children's whining and complaining? Who *really* makes the rules around your house? How can you make sure you remain the leader, regardless of how popular you might be at any one time?

♦ In what ways do you like to be served rather than to serve your family? How can you counteract this tendency? In what ways can you pitch in at home to help your loved ones? What kind of assistance do they most need and want from you? How are you teaching your family to become an effective team? What kind of an example do you present in the area of teamwork?

♦ In what ways do we often take prayer lightly? Do you see prayer as one of the most important ways you can serve your family? How does a regular prayer life help you to admit your inadequacy as a father and to secure the help you need?

♦ How can Hannah's example help you as a father? What does it mean to you to give your little ones to the Lord? How are you bringing up your children in the faith? Who is helping you in this task? Who can help you become a better spiritual example for your children?

DADS IN THE BIBLE

It's one of the most awful stories in the Old Testament, but it's in there for a reason. A dad named Achan made a conscious decision to disobey God. His defiance and willful foolishness cost him not only his own life, but the lives of each member of his family. Read about Achan and the things you and I can learn on page 226.

A CLOSING PRAYER

Have someone in your group ask each man, "How can we pray for you this week?" As usual, write down each of these requests so that each member of your group can remember them in his own daily times of prayer. End your time together with a prayer, either with someone praying spontaneously or by offering the following prayer:

Dear Father in heaven, thank You for sending us the Holy Spirit, the Helper. How we need Your help! You have given us a big job, but You have also given us everything we need to succeed. Remind us to ask for the assistance we require, whether from a pastor, a friend, a coach, a teacher, or our wives. The task is big, but You are bigger. Thank you. Amen.

YOUR CLOSETFUL OF HATS

DAY ONE: THE BIG PICTURE

My dad was a hat man. Who knows how this happened? Maybe his dad was also a guy who never went outside without a hatted head. Or maybe it was his high-control mother—and he *did* have one—who determined that a covered head protected a boy against dive-bombing germs. Regardless, Samuel Wolgemuth did headgear.

When he went to heaven in February 2002, my five siblings and I each delivered short eulogies in his honor. I chose to talk about the hats, even bringing a boxful of them to the pulpit with me. And as I talked about the many roles my father played in his life, I'd put on a hat to make the point visual as well as verbal. There was a baseball cap because that clearly was his favorite team sport and one he excelled in as a kid. He loved to hit fly balls to my brothers and me in the big, vacant lot behind our boyhood home.

There was the NAPA cap. Dad called himself "a shade tree mechanic." And until he got too old to nimbly maneuver under a hood (or cars became essentially laptop computers with axles—I honestly don't remember which came first), my dad loved to work on his car. In fact, even though he was a clergyman, dad owned a chain of auto parts stores in Pennsylvania. Anyway, these hats became symbols of the things my dad did. They represented the sharp corners of the man.

Even if the only hats you and I wear are worn and filthy baseball caps—the caps our wives would like to declare condemned as chemical spill sites—we

71

love to don them when we're working outside on the weekend. The point is obvious. Whether we actually put them on our heads or not, you and I wear a lot of hats. Husband, dad, neighbor, employee, son, employer, comforter, brother, churchman, coach, volunteer, lawn boy, psychologist, garbage man, handyman . . .

When you and I consider the size of our calling as a dad, the job can look gargantuan, even overwhelming. And when we consider the many roles every father has to play (we'll briefly look at four of the most important, but as I've just listed, there are more), the task can seem nearly impossible. But don't let your gaze stop with the job description; let it go far beyond that. Look instead for the fresh perspective that comes with knowing that God is with you and that He has promised to strengthen you, guide you, and fit you—get it?—for the task ahead. Yes, it's a big job; but you and I have a far bigger God who declares His eagerness to walk alongside, helping with every hat.

OH AND ONE MORE THING . . .

♦ You may not be much of a hat man, but you still wear a lot of them. What are some of the most important hats you wear? Sometimes it takes a submissive spirit to ask for help in donning them all. Listen to this: "Be humble under God's powerful hand so he will lift you up when the right time comes. Give all your worries to him, because he cares about you" (1 Peter 5:7, page 1319). God is a great help with those hats! Who are the people you count on to help you with putting on your hats?

♦ PROVIDER ♦

DAY TWO: READ 1 TIMOTHY 5:8 (PAGE 1281)

Every dad feels pressure to supply his family's needs. That's a natural, God-given thing, designed to help us fulfill our role as provider. But our culture's endless promotion of material things often intensifies this pressure to desperately unhealthy levels. How can we consider our job complete if we "only" furnish the basics of food, clothing, and shelter? What about the latest electronic gadgets, designer athletic shoes, cars when they turn sixteen, and a vacation home on the beach?

Don't be fooled. Your finest gift to your family is *you*—your time, your presence, your affection, and especially, your love. Lots and lots of love! Your job is to mirror in a small way God's provision for you. And what is God's greatest gift to you?

Himself.

Think of it like this. Your children came into the world with nothing. As their dad, you serve their needs. Even when they give you nothing of negotiable value in return, you work hard to give them the food, shelter, clothing, and other essentials. It makes you happy to do these things because you love your kids.

That, on a small scale, is just how your Father in heaven treats you. He comes to you in your need when you have nothing to give Him in return. And He doesn't parcel out mere table scraps; He lavishes on you the best he has to offer. Abundant life and spiritual nourishment are yours for the taking. Best of all, He gives you Himself. And why does He so lavishly provide for you? Because He loves you.

♦ What dimensions of being your family's provider create the most pressure for you? How do you respond to this pressure? How can others help you deal with it?

73

♦ How are you doing at giving your family ample amounts of: (a) time; (b) your presence; (c) your affection; (d) your love? Where are you doing well? Where do you need improvement? What kind of outside support do you think you could most use?

♦ Comment on the following quote: "Your job is to mirror in a small way God's provision for you." How does God provide for you? List some ways. How can you mirror this provision for your family?

♦ How does love differ from other motivators as a reason to give your best to your family? How do you show your love through this effort? What areas may suffer from a deficit of love?

◆ DISCIPLINARIAN ◆

DAY THREE: READ GENESIS 2:17 (PAGE 3)

The garden of Eden was beautiful and perfect in every way. The man had a tender and loving relationship with the woman; the woman respected the man. They lived with one another, and with God, without dissension or fear. They enjoyed impeccable relationships.

Amazingly, right in the middle of this pristine flawlessness, stood a "no." God told the man and woman that they could not eat of the fruit of a centrally located, exquisite tree.

Most of the time, I think of enjoyment as having no boundaries, no inhibitions. I want it, I get it, and no one stops me. Sounds great, doesn't it? But God, knowing us better than we know ourselves, has created us with a need for discipline and boundaries. We feel most happy with certain restrictions and guidelines placed before us.

Sometimes, being a dad can be a drag. You feel like the house policeman, prosecuting attorney, and judge, all rolled into one. Take heart! Remember that even Eden, God's perfect garden, included some discipline. Your family members may never celebrate your discipline—but they are happier with it than they would be without it.

◆ How can you best balance fatherly generosity (the desire to say "yes") with fatherly discipline (saying "no" when necessary)? How can you know when to say "yes" and when to say "no"? What specific principles guide you?

75

♦ To what kinds of things in your family may God want you to say "no"?

♦ What benefits do your children receive from your willingness to tell them "no", when necessary? What benefits would they lack if you never told them "no"?

♦ When is it hardest for you to say "no" to your child? Why do you suppose this is true?

♦ How do you handle it when your child responds to your "no" with questioning, resistance, or rebellion?

♦ COMMUNICATOR ♦

DAY FOUR: READ GENESIS 45:15 (PAGE 57)

The most precious connection between human beings is the bridge of conversation. This is especially true between you and your children.

If you have small children, communication can be difficult. You live in a world totally foreign to your young son or daughter. While you feel pressure at work and sometimes struggle to make ends meet, she has a dolly who scraped her knee or mud on his tricycle wheels. How do you find common ground to discuss your very different lives and somehow bring them closer together?

Early on, a good friend advised me, "On the weekends, never go anywhere alone." This simple advice had wonderful consequences. When I ran errands on the weekends, I almost always took one or both of my kids along. As we drove to the store, I'd ask questions. "Look in that field. Have you ever seen so many cows?" They'd look and start counting. "Look at all the windows in that building. How many do you think there are?"

I would ask them about their lives. "What do you love most about church?" Or, "What's your favorite thing about mom?" (You're welcome to add your favorite thing about her, too.)

Or we'd play games: "If you were an animal, which one would you like to be?" We began to build conversation bridges, a connection of words that bound us together. This began teaching them at an early age to share their thoughts freely and openly.

As children get older, this bridge of conversation will enable you to honestly and openly discuss their problems and personal issues. How will your sixteen-year-old ever talk to you about an uncomfortable verbal bout with a classmate unless he learned to have such discussions with you as a young child, when the stakes were not so high?

Teach your kids to talk to you. Open conversation will serve as a lifeline that keeps your kids from emotionally hiding from you. It will allow you to learn who your children really are and will give you a vehicle to tell them about yourself. Teaching your children the art of conversation also will introduce them to a world of other adults who will honor them because of their ability to both talk and to listen.

♦ How do you try to find common ground with your children and somehow bring their worlds and yours together?

♦ Would the suggestion, "On the weekends, never go anywhere alone," work for you in building bridges of communication with your children?

♦ What is your plan for teaching your children the art of communication?

♦ What adults can you introduce into your children's world that will help your kids learn how to relate and converse with grown-ups outside of your family? How can you encourage conversations between your kids and these adults?

♦ INITIATOR OF AFFECTION ♦

DAY FIVE: READ MARK 10:16 (PAGE 1053)

One of the greatest privileges you have as a dad is the opportunity to shower affection on your children. One crucial way to do this is through tender touch.

Hold your children when they're tiny, and stroke their faces with your hand. Hold their hands when they learn to walk. Visit their rooms just before they go to sleep, scratch their backs, and kiss them good night. Hug them with your whole arms—wrap them up as if they're in a blanket. Let their hearts know that they are absolutely secure in their daddy's arms.

As they grow older, the kinds of touch might change, but the message remains the same. Find ways to continue to show them that, even as they become more independent and move toward adulthood, you are still there to love and protect them.

Of course, all of this touching takes extra time. Meaningful touch doesn't happen on the fly. You have to slow down to make it count.

Hug your son. Gently tug your daughter toward you for a warm embrace. Stop running; take a moment, and touch your children.

♦ At the current age(s) of your child(ren), what kinds of affection do you feel have the best chance to communicate genuine and pure love?

♦ What kind of "meaningful touch" did your parents share with you? How did this affect you? Did your experience as a child help or hamper you as an adult?

♦ Do you agree that "meaningful touch doesn't happen on the fly" and that "you have to slow down to make it count"?

♦ Tell some stories about your best memories, as a dad, involving meaningful affection with your children.

HUDDLE UP: FOR GROUP DISCUSSION

Look back over your notes from this past week, and share one or two things that felt especially significant to you.

The following questions will help your group to review:

♦ Which of your many hats do you consider the most challenging? Which are the most fulfilling? Which do you need the most help with?

♦ How would you describe your role as provider? What kind of pressure do you feel in this role? Why is it so hard to remember, sometimes, that the best gift you can give your family is the gift of yourself? What can God teach you about this most important provision of giving yourself?

♦ How would you describe yourself as a disciplinarian? What kinds of boundaries do you set for your family? What do you find hardest about saying no to your children? Why are your children happier with your discipline than without it?

♦ How effective do you think you are as a communicator with your family members? How do you use communication to bridge differing worlds? What can you do to encourage free and open sharing of thoughts? How are you teaching your children the art of communication?

♦ In what ways are you your family's initiator of affection? What place does tender touch have in your relationship with your family members? How secure do your loved ones feel in your arms? How do you find the extra time that meaningful touch requires? When did you last give everyone in your home a warm embrace?

DADS IN THE BIBLE

We don't know what Noah did for a living before God told him to build the ark, but it's for sure that his "boat builder" hat was a surprise addition to his closet. Read about Noah on page 9.

A CLOSING PRAYER

Invite someone to ask every member of your group, "How can we pray for you this week?" By writing down each request, every man can remember these needs during his own daily prayer time. We suggest that you conclude your session by asking a volunteer to offer an impromptu prayer, or someone could speak aloud the suggested prayer below:

Dear Father in heaven, You know all about wearing a lot of hats—more than we ever will. When we begin to feel overwhelmed with all the responsibilities of fatherhood, help us to remember that You are our Father . . . and that You want to partner with us to help us succeed in this great adventure of being a dad. Thank you. Amen.

6

THE GREENHOUSE EFFECT

DAY ONE: THE BIG PICTURE

Over the past several years, a scientific argument has broken out regarding the effects of CO_2 and global warming. Normally docile—and very smart—experts have come to the brink of public fistfights over this issue. Not to worry! This isn't the "greenhouse effect" we're going to talk about this week.

Just outside of Wheaton, Illinois, where I grew up, stood miles and miles of long, glass buildings. (Or, as a kid, speeding along the country road in the car with my dad, it *seemed* like "miles and miles.") These structures were, in fact, greenhouses that harbored thousands of growing plants. Even though many of these plants could have survived fairly well outside, the greenhouses guaranteed them an ideal climate. Every day. The owners of the greenhouses knew how to create the perfect environment for their plants to grow strong and beautiful.

Your home and mine are greenhouses. The plants are our kids. No, actually, the plants are our kids' hearts.

To be perfectly honest, you may be pushing back on this metaphor. "I don't want my home to protect my kids from reality," you might argue. "They need to experience the treacheries of life at home so the realities of the outside world don't blow them away."

I understand what you're saying. I really do. So let me take another run at it.

The power of a greenhouse lies in its environment, intentionally created by its owner. In a similar way, the power of a good home lies in the healthy environment intentionally created by the dad and mom.

In Deuteronomy 19:1–13 (page 201), God instructed Moses to establish "cities of safety" as designated locations for innocent people wrongly accused of premeditated murder. These cities did not exist to shelter real criminals; the law applied here just like everywhere else. They simply were places where people knew that truth reigned, regardless of the neighborhood or school-yard buzz about them. This is the kind of greenhouse your home can be.

Imagine a home where the truth about you and your kids was all that mattered, a place where no one pretended to be someone else and where no one jumped to premature and inaccurate conclusions about their identity. In such a place, you could be who you really are without any pressure to appear like someone else. Here you and your kids would be loved and appreciated, not because of your utility or capability, but simply *because*.

This is exactly what your home should feel like to each member of your family. Your home needs to be a place of refuge, a tender place of welcome and safety. A dwelling where there's no need for pretense and no plastic reward for performance; where the inhabitants inside find nurture without suffocation, discipline without disrespect, and love without limits.

That's the kind of greenhouse we're talking about.

OH, AND ONE MORE THING . . .

Assuming that you're going along with me on the greenhouse metaphor . . .

♦ What outside forces in your world create the need for a place of "safety"? From what dangers do you and your family need protection?

DAY TWO: READ DEUTERONOMY 4:29 (PAGE 187)

Can there be a higher goal for our households than to be occupied by people who seek God? Moses reminded the Israelites that their new life in the promised land would continue to be all about following God . . . knowing and reading His Word, listening carefully for His voice, obeying His directions, and most of all, loving Him wholeheartedly. And then He gave them an incredible promise: "You can look for the Lord your God, and you will find him if you look for him with your whole being." Can there be a greater reward than finding God? I don't think so.

Think of it this way. Whose hand would you most like to shake? Whose autograph would you most love to have? Imagine that you just walked into your favorite restaurant, and *that* person—the one you were just thinking about—is standing right there, waiting for a table. Tingles run from the top of your head to the soles of your feet. Your heart races and your hands get clammy. Without succumbing to the temptation of acting like a junior high rock-star groupie, you gather the courage to introduce yourself. And for a few fleeting seconds, you enjoy the company of your hero.

Now consider that our God has no equal. He is incomparable. His greatness and power and respectability and wisdom make our human "hero" as ordinary as the mailman. (If *you're* a mailman, I'm *sure* you're extraordinary.)

So take a deep breath. We have the honor of introducing our children to *this* One.

♦ Who are your "heroes"? Who would you most like to meet? Why? How would you compare your excitement at meeting them with your enthusiasm for meeting with God?

♦ How much time does your household spend in "seeking God?" How much of a priority have you made it?

♦ In what ways do you lead your family in actively seeking God? Are you satisfied with your leadership in this area?

♦ What strategies are you employing to introduce your children to Jesus Christ?

DAY THREE: READ ROMANS 3:21–24 (PAGE 1194)

Paul's words to the church in Rome should stop us in our tracks: "*Every-one* has sinned and fallen short of God's glorious standard" (v. 23, emphasis added). Thankfully, we can "be made right with God by his grace, which is a free gift . . . through Jesus Christ" (v. 24).

Dads who speak only of *one* of these two truths to their children are making a monumental error. If all they talk about is falling short of perfection, then their kids will know only that they are sinners and their conduct may stoop to match this low self-image. On the other hand, dads who talk only about grace eliminate their chances to bring needed discipline and structure to their children. No discipline equals no joy.

As dads, we have a twofold responsibility. It's imperative that our children understand that they are sinners and that sin has dire consequences. But we must also help them understand what it means to be justified before a holy God—that when they place their faith in Jesus, they're counted as innocent because of God's loving grace. Together, these two truths can serve as your best guide in leading your kids to their own rich and satisfying relationships with God.

♦ How do you explain to your children the truth of their sinfulness (Romans 3:23, page 1194)? What illustrations or pictures seem to be most effective?

♦ How do you explain to your children the truth of God's grace (Ephesians 2:8, 9, page 1250)? How have they responded to this message?

♦ Which of these two truths do you more naturally emphasize? How can you bring more balance to this?

♦ What do your kids know about having a relationship with God? What do they understand about Jesus Christ's role in making such a relationship possible?

DAY FOUR: READ ROMANS 7:7–12 (PAGE 1199)

The most important tool in your workshop is your tape measure; without it (and the accurate and unchanging standards it represents), nothing you create will turn out right. In a similar way, the Bible is like your tape measure for your life of faith: it reveals God's unchanging standard for you as God's child.

The Scripture provides for all humankind a trustworthy statement of what is right and wrong. God's law shows us how far from the mark we have fallen. It also gives us a picture of how to get back on track.

When a man's children are small—and before they personally experience the truth and discipline of God's law as revealed by his Spirit—they need someone to show them the right way to live. That someone is you. It's a dad's responsibility to show his family what God's standards have shown him: the value of personal confession, trusting faith, and the Father's grace.

Most of what your children learn of God's Word, of course, will be *caught* more than *taught*. Because this is true, let them frequently catch you in God's Word. Love what He instructs you to love. Let your children overhear you expressing genuine appreciation for your church and for those in leadership there. Involve your family in faithfully praying for friends and family, for elected officials, for strangers in need. Through your example, let them experience the Bible as a living book that makes a genuine difference in their lives of faith.

♦ How is the Bible like a spiritual tape measure?

♦ How have you used the Bible to focus your family's attention on: (1) the value of personal confession; (b) trusting faith; (c) the Father's grace?

♦ How often do your children "catch" you in God's Word? Do they see it on your lap when your minister is preaching? What do they learn from your example about a proper attitude toward church, toward prayer, and toward other spiritual disciplines laid out in Scripture? (Solitude: Matthew 6:6, page 998; Simplicity: Matthew 6:1–4; Study: 2 Timothy 2:15, page 1284; Service: Galatians 5:13, page 1246.)

♦ How have you experienced the Bible as a living book that makes a genuine difference in your own life of faith?

DAY FIVE: Read Proverbs 22:1–6 (page 661)

Sometimes you may feel tempted to sell your children on *your* dreams for them rather than help them to dream their *own*. Sometimes they feel pressure to become what you want them to be. Of course, you want the best for your kids, so it can be tough to avoid this temptation. But it's even tougher for kids who grow up under such parental stress.

Several years ago, during lunch, a close friend said something I'll never forget. "I'm a grown man," he said. "I have two children, two cars, a career, and a mortgage of my own. And I've just discovered that all I have done is become *exactly* what my parents wanted me to become. I have no idea who *I* am."

Don't allow this to happen to your kids. Don't try to get them to follow your agenda. Your job is to expose them to different options, to encourage them to pursue their own dreams, to discover what God may have for them, and then to do whatever you can to help them succeed.

Being an effective dad does not mean creating someone who grows up to be a clone of yourself. The goal is not aiming your children at *your* target. Rather, being a good dad means helping your children move in the direction God leads them to go. Teach them to listen for His voice and follow Him for their own callings, gifts, and strengths.

♦ What dreams and hopes do you have for your children? How could any of these stand in the way of God's best for them?

♦ How are you exposing your children to the many options they have and encouraging them to pursue their own dreams as they dovetail with God's direction? How have you let them know that you're there to help them succeed?

♦ How can you help your children identify and follow their own callings and to develop their unique strengths and interests?

♦ What specifically can you do to help your children learn how to listen for God's voice, identify his thoughts, and pursue His leading?

HUDDLE UP: FOR GROUP DISCUSSION

Look back over your notes from this past week, and share one or two things that seemed especially significant to you.

The following questions will help your group to review:

♦ In what ways is your home like a "city of safety"? In what ways is it not? How can you increasingly make your home into a tender place of welcome and security? How can you make your home a dwelling where there is no need for pretense and no reward for performance; where the inhabitants inside find nurture without suffocation, discipline without disrespect, and love without limits?

♦ How do your kids see you seeking God as the highest goal for your life? How are you providing your children with a model of what it means to love God wholeheartedly? What might be some effective ways to introduce your children to God? What have you already tried?

♦ What does it mean to "fall short" of God's "glory"? Why is this a big deal? How can someone be made right in God's sight? What is the relationship between grace and faith? What crucial twofold responsibility do you have as a dad? How can you prepare your children to secure and enjoy a rich and fulfilling relationship with God?

♦ In what way is the Bible like a tape measure? How does the Bible show you what is morally right and wrong? How can you use the Bible to show someone how to get back on a right track with God? Why is faith more caught than taught? How can you help your children to "catch" their own faith in Christ?

♦ How can you help your children pursue their dreams, under God, rather than your dreams for them? Why is it such a temptation to try to make clones of yourself? How can you expose your children to various options within God's will? How can you help your children hit the target God has laid out for them?

DADS IN THE BIBLE

David's son Solomon provides us with a strong example of a greenhouse-owning dad. Solomon wrote a whole book (Proverbs) to set the environment for his own kids and generations to follow. He got direct instruction from his dad for the kind of man he should be . . . things like, "Be a good and strong leader. Obey the Lord your God" (1 Kings 2:2, 3, page 342). Read about Solomon on page 636.

A CLOSING PRAYER

Have someone in your group ask each man, "How can we pray for you this week?" Remember to write down each request, so every group member can refer to these requests in his own daily prayers. To end your time together, you might ask a volunteer to pray for the group, or you could have someone read aloud the following suggested prayer:

Dear Father in heaven, what an amazing privilege it is to be called Your children. And what an awesome responsibility it is to be given the opportunity to help lead our own children to faith in Jesus. Lord, help us to be faithful in this most sacred of duties. Give us wisdom, love, and grace as we represent You to our kids. And thank You, Lord, for reassuring us that You love our children more than we ever could. Amen.

◆ NOTES ◆

PICK ME, PICK ME

DAY ONE: THE BIG PICTURE

The vacant field behind my boyhood home in Illinois was just the right size for play. Neighbor boys and my brothers and I would gather in warm weather for a pickup game of touch football. Or softball.

Two boys got picked randomly as captains, beginning the draft process. The highest went first to enthusiastic cheers; the lowest went last with shrugged resignation.

Because my testosterone hovered on the shady side of the launchpad until I turned sixteen, I often was one of the smaller boys on the field. Celebration did not break out when someone called my name. More often than not, in fact, my name didn't need to be called at all. When you're picked last, names don't matter much.

I remember longing for the day someone would choose *me*.
Pick me! Pick me!

Forty-five years later, I'm sitting in a noisy auditorium in Charlotte, North Carolina. Parents, grandparents and friends, filled with anticipation, file in to their assigned seats. My wife and I wait in the subdued light for the start of the Arborbrook Christian School musical. Tonight the students will perform excerpts from the Broadway musical *Annie*. Our granddaughter, Abby, has the lead.

You remember the story: a precocious, redheaded orphan during the time of the Great Depression; a mean-tempered spinster, Miss Agatha Hannigan, in charge of the girls at the Municipal Orphanage . . . and a single and very wealthy industrialist tycoon named Mr. Oliver Warbucks. Eventually, the little girl gets noticed; then she's loved, and finally adopted by Warbucks. Annie moves into the man's spacious and opulent Fifth Avenue mansion as his daughter.

I saw the original Broadway production in the late '70s, but this rendition was *far* superior. And you know why. Good thing I had slipped an extra handkerchief into my pocket on my way out the door!

Not incidentally, the play ends on Christmas morning, when everyone agrees that this is the start of a wonderful new life.

A homeless and hopeless child, an indescribably wealthy man . . . and an adoption. No longer penniless and afraid, Annie literally becomes Warbucks' child—and heir to his untold riches. Even more satisfying than getting drafted in the first round on the vacant lot behind our house, an unworthy person is chosen to become the child of the richest man in New York City. What a great story.

Pick me! Pick me!

Now listen to these words from the pen of the apostle Paul:

> For as many as are led by the Spirit of God, these are sons of God. For you did not receive the spirit of bondage again to fear, but you received the Spirit of adoption by whom we cry out, "Abba, Father." The Spirit Himself bears witness with our spirit that we are children of God, and if children, then heirs—heirs of God and joint heirs with Christ. (Romans 8:14–17 NKJV).

The God of the universe, the One who created everything by the power of His spoken word, chose you and me to be His sons. By the choice of our sovereign, heavenly Father, we have been adopted and have become legal heirs to the kind of riches that make Oliver Warbucks' wealth look like chump change.

Hearing my name called first for pickup football can't compare. My own bedroom in a Fifth Street mansion is no match. By an act of His will, I am God's *son*. And so are you . . . my brother.

OH, AND ONE MORE THING . . .

Like the prophet Jeremiah, you and I were handpicked to be adopted before we were even conceived: "Before I made you in your mother's womb, I chose you. Before you were born, I set you apart for a special work" (Jeremiah 1:5, page 770).

No need to ask Him to pick us. He has already chosen us to be His beloved sons. Adopted into His family at His own good pleasure. Handpicked.

Isn't this amazing?

♦ What does it feel like to be passed by . . . like the last kid to be picked for a game, or an orphan nobody loves? Since you and I are neither of these, what does the opposite feel like? How should this fact affect *everything*?

DAY TWO: READ 1 SAMUEL 2:12–26 (PAGE 278)

For this final week of our study together, we're going to look at four dads in the Bible. Their lives are not only interesting, but they also provide a template for you and me to follow—or to avoid. First, an Old Testament priest named Eli.

The Bible calls Eli's sons "evil men" who "did not care about the Lord." The text tells us they tampered with the nation's sacred religious rituals and seduced the women who served as ushers in the tabernacle.

Inevitably—because fathers eventually do find out what's going on—the aging Eli, a priest in the temple, called his sons together. "Why do you do these evil things that people tell me about?" he asked (v. 23). But Eli's wild sons felt unmoved by their aged father's whining.

As his boys grew up, Eli probably kept a very busy schedule; you know how this feels. The demands on our time as dads can feel relentless. Unfortunately, Eli evidently had used up his wisdom and good judgment at the office. When he arrived home, he had nothing left for his most important charge ... his own family.

Eli's failure as a father provides a bitter reminder that a man's most important task is the consistent, thankless, and at times, painful regulation of his own household. Other things in life—a successful career, sports, a committee, even serving at church—may seem more rewarding or significant. But don't be fooled. Eli's error ultimately cost his boys their lives. Passivity in the home carries a staggering price.

♦ We're introduced to Eli's sons as "men," so we have nothing to observe about their lives as youngsters. Could Eli have done more to restrain these men, or by that time in their lives, was it too late?

♦ Why is passivity at home such a problem for so many men? Does it ever tempt you?

♦ How often does your busy schedule keep you from interacting as much as you should with your children at home? How have you dealt with this problem?

♦ Describe (without giving his name) a dad you know whose home life suffers because of his passivity . . . or his schedule. What, if anything, can concerned friends do in such a situation?

DAY THREE: READ 1 KINGS 11:11–13 (PAGE 355)

For many years our neighbor faithfully applied top-quality, weed-killing chemicals to his lawn. His yard looked like a page out of a magazine, vibrantly green and dandelion-free. When this neighbor moved, the new owner told us that he hadn't been "a lawn guy" in the past, but since he now owned the lawn of the county, he intended to change his ways.

The former owner protected his lawn from weeds. When the new owner moved in, he had a choice. He could either keep up the horticultural regimen and enjoy the benefits, or discontinue it and allow the weeds to quickly multiply.

King David reminds me of my former neighbor. By confessing his sin and turning to the Lord in obedience, he benefited not only himself during his lifetime, but he also supplied a hedge of protection for his son, Solomon, after his death.

As a dad, you have a responsibility to be God's man—at work, at home, and in the quietness of your own heart. This choice will bring tangible dividends to you during your lifetime, especially the great joy of experiencing reconciliation with God. But this isn't the only benefit you will reap from living a godly life. By your example, you will protect your children as well—killing the weeds in their lawns, so to speak—long after you are gone.

And thousands of years from now, in one of God's heavenly books, perhaps it will be said of you as it is said of David in the Bible, "[Your name] did God's will during his lifetime" (Acts 13:36, page 1169). When God writes such glowing words for your epitaph, you're a blessed man, for sure. And so are your children.

♦ What does your own lawn say about you and your personal traits? What parallels, if any, do you see between it and your spiritual life?

♦ What kind of "hedge of protection" are you building for your children? What choices might you need to make to strengthen that hedge?

♦ What does it mean to you to be "God's man" in your family? In your neighborhood? At work? What benefits are there from choosing to live a godly life?

♦ How would you like to be remembered after you're gone? If you were to die tonight, how do you think people would recall your life, your job as a dad, and your relationship with God?

DAY FOUR: READ MARK 9:14–27 (PAGE 1050)

Year after year, a father with a demon-possessed son agonized over his boy's heartbreaking malady. Imagine the overpowering distress and confusion he must have felt. "Let him break his arm or contract a bad case of the flu," he might have pleaded with God, "but please, not *this* awful thing." Still, the more he tried to help his son, the worse his boy's condition grew.

This father lived in the hollow space between unbelief and belief. He was no cynic. He believed his boy could be healed, but he had done everything he knew to do. When Jesus' disciples approached his home, one more time he gathered up his courage and brought his afflicted child to these men, whom he hoped could help. But none of them could drive out the demon.

One more failed attempt.

You can feel the anguish of this desperate, frustrated dad. When Jesus arrived, He tried to draw out the man's faith by asking him to give a public witness to his faith. "I do believe," the weary dad replied. But then he added: "Help me to believe more!" (v. 24). He knew that his faith had its limits, something that every honest man would surely admit.

We know how Jesus responded to this broken man's request. Mark wrote, "Jesus took hold of the boy's hand and helped him to stand up" (v. 27). And at the same time—perhaps for the first time ever—the persevering father's wobbly faith stood to its feet as well.

♦ How badly do you want your child to be "healed"? What's it worth to you to see him or her walk in the truth? What are you willing to do to have your son or daughter follow God?

♦ Carefully read the text in Mark. Although Jesus noted the lack of faith in both this unnamed man and in His disciples, He was clearly more harsh with one than with the other. Who got the harsher rebuke, and why?

♦ Describe the most serious difficulties you have faced with your children, when nothing seemed to help. What did you do? What help did you seek out?

♦ According to this story, how much faith does it take to get Jesus' attention and intervention? Does this encourage you?

DAY FIVE: Read Psalm 103 (page 607)

Have you ever tried to sympathize with a child's trouble or patch up a scuffed knee without squatting down and stooping to his or her level? It's, frankly, impossible. Unless a child sees the understanding on your face, and unless he or she sees you down on his or her level, that child won't be able to understand or even accept the comfort you try to offer.

God demonstrates exactly this kind of care for His children. Our Father takes moments from His busy schedule—keeping the stars and planets on their charted courses, growing food for a hungry world, reminding us to blink every few seconds, raising up and bringing down world leaders—to stoop to our level and have compassion on His bumped and bruised children.

Jesus reinforced the psalmist's observation when He said, "Two sparrows cost only a penny, but not even one of them can die without your Father's knowing it . . . So don't be afraid. You are worth much more than many sparrows" (Matthew 10:29, 31, page 1005).

You're a busy man. You've got places to go, people to see, deals to get done. As the Creator of all there is, God is extremely busy too . . . and yet He has tremendous compassion. He's never too busy to stop, never too proud to stoop. It's a good thing, too. How else could we ever see His face?

Look carefully; this Father has *lots* of love. He stops; then He stoops. And He calls and empowers you and me to follow in His compassionate footsteps.

♦ How well do you think you sympathize with your child's hurts and challenges? When have you been most effective at showing your child compassion?

◆ How do you "stoop" to your child's level, either when he or she needs some special comfort or on an ordinary day? What do you normally do?

◆ Why do you think Jesus thought it was important to tell us that God believes we're worth more than "many sparrows"? What is the point? How does this point apply to your fathering?

◆ God combines an extremely busy schedule with an extraordinarily compassionate heart. What can you do to follow His example?

Huddle Up: For Group Discussion

Look back over your notes from this past week, and share one or two things that seemed especially meaningful to you.

The following questions will help your group to review:

♦ How can you be God's man in your family? What choices does this entail? What sort of "hedge of protection" would you like to build for your family? How can you go about building it? What benefits from living a godly life have you already enjoyed? What kind of benefits would you like to pass along to your children, and their children?

♦ What sorts of stubborn problems do you face with your children? What have you tried so far that hasn't seemed to work? How can you relate to the father who inhabited a "hollow space between belief and unbelief"? What are you willing to do to see your child follow God? How has Jesus been using difficulties to build your faith?

♦ In what ways is God the ultimate Father? How has He stooped to your level to bring you help and comfort? How can you better follow His example? Regardless of the ages of your children, how can you squat down and stoop to their level to bring them your understanding and compassion?

A CLOSING PRAYER

Have someone in your group ask each man, "How can we pray for you this week?" As everyone shares their requests, encourage one another to write them down so you all can better pray for them in the coming week.

Finally, close your time together with a time of spontaneous prayer, or have someone read aloud the following suggested prayer:

Dear Father in heaven, what an amazing privilege it is to call you "Father." You created the universe, and You continue to uphold all things by the power of Your word—and yet every day You stop and stoop to our level, to show us Your compassion and to lavish on us Your love. Help us, Father, to do the same for our families. Make us into men of compassion and dads of deep, abiding love. We love you, Lord. And we are grateful. Amen.

♦ FINAL NOTE ♦

If you would like to read some suggested answers to all the questions in *The Father's Plan* study guide, you can find them on www.robertwolgemuth.com. These are not meant to be the only right answers for every situation, but they may guide you as you study, sparking some ideas for your own answers or keeping you from getting stuck. I hope they provide some help to you.

✦ EPILOGUE ✦

THOU SHALT SMILE

One day a pastor was making calls on senior citizen members who were often unable to attend worship services. One of his favorites was a little old lady living in a small frame house on a pristine, shady street. Widowed and spry, she was amazingly energetic for her age, optimistic, generous, with flashing crystal blue eyes . . . and a heart of gold. The pastor sat down on the large, slip-covered chair at the end of the coffee table. She sat at the end of the couch just across the corner.

Impulsively and without asking, the pastor reached into the dish of peanuts—a true weakness of the man—positioned within reach on the coffee table. The lady didn't seem to notice. The two talked freely about life and family and the church. Finished with the peanuts in his hand, the pastor reached into the bowl again . . . and again and again until it was empty, save for a few stray peanut crumbs on the bottom.

As though completely surprised by what he had done, the pastor recoiled in horror. "I cannot believe that I have eaten all your peanuts," he said. "I didn't mean to."

But the expression of his companion only brightened. "That's okay," she said, her eyes dancing. "I hate peanuts."

Relieved, the pastor sighed a great sigh. But the lady wasn't quite finished.

"But I love that chocolate coating they put on them," she continued. "And I've sucked them all clean."

This Epilogue is like the candy dish on your grandmother's coffee table . . . and, unlike our sweet little old lady with the crystal blue eyes, no one has had their way with any of the candies before you get to them.

When you and I walk past the dish on the coffee table, we may reach down and take just a few. Then we keep walking. We don't stop, stoop down to the table, and stay there until all the candies are gone. Unlike the pastor, we don't take the goodies by the multiple handful. No, these treats are only to sweeten your journey through the living room.

This Epilogue is that candy dish, and the few pages that follow are the treats inside. They're not meant to be eaten all at once (although you *can* if you want). They're only meant to enhance your important journey through *The Father's Plan* study guide. Every once in a while, whether you are coming or going, these may be just the quick and sweet treat you're looking for. There are no hidden meanings tucked away. No subliminal Old Testament prophecies hiding there.

Just something fun to stop, pick up, and pop into your brain. Just for a smile.

SOME LAWYER FUN

These are alleged to be transcripts of actual conversations between attorneys and witnesses in court. If you're a lawyer, my apologies . . . sort of.

ATTORNEY: This amnesia, does it affect your memory at all?
WITNESS: Yes.
ATTORNEY: And in what ways does it affect your memory?
WITNESS: I forget.
ATTORNEY: You forget? Can you give us an example of something you
    forgot?

ATTORNEY: She had three children, right?
WITNESS: Yes.
ATTORNEY: How many were boys?
WITNESS: None.
ATTORNEY: Were there any girls?
WITNESS: Your Honor, I think I need a different attorney. Can I get a new
    attorney?

ATTORNEY: Can you describe the individual?

WITNESS: He was about medium height and had a beard.

ATTORNEY: Was this a male or a female?

WITNESS: Unless the circus was in town I'm going with male.

ATTORNEY: Doctor, before you performed the autopsy, did you check for a pulse?

WITNESS: No.

ATTORNEY: Did you check for blood pressure?

WITNESS: No.

ATTORNEY: Did you check for breathing?

WITNESS: No.

ATTORNEY: So, then it is possible that the patient was alive when you began the autopsy?

WITNESS: No.

ATTORNEY: How can you be so sure, Doctor?

WITNESS: Because his brain was sitting on my desk in a jar.

ATTORNEY: I see, but could the patient have still been alive, nevertheless?

WITNESS: Yes, it is possible that he could have been alive and practicing law.

Aphorisms

Aph·o·rism [af-uh-riz-uhm] a terse saying embodying a general truth, or astute observation.

- ◆ Money will buy a fine dog, but only kindness will make him wag his tail.

- ◆ If you don't have a sense of humor, you probably don't have any sense at all.

- ◆ A good time to keep your mouth shut is when you're in deep water.

- Why does it take so little time for a child who is afraid of the dark to become a teenager who wants to stay out all night?

- Business conventions are important because they demonstrate how many people a company can operate without.

- Scratch a cat and you will have a permanent job.

- No one has more driving ambition than the boy who wants to buy a car.

- No one ever says it's only a game when their team is winning.

FORE!

Only a true golfer will understand or appreciate these.[1] If you're not, please turn the page. If you are or you aspire to be, enjoy.

- Don't buy a putter until you've had a chance to throw it.

- Never try to keep more than three hundred separate thoughts in your mind during your swing.

- When your shot has to carry over a water hazard, you can either hit one more club or two more balls.

- If you're afraid a full shot might reach the green while the foursome ahead of you is still putting out, you have two options: you can immediately shank a lay-up or you can wait until the green is clear and top a ball halfway there.

- The less skilled the player, the more likely he is to share his ideas about your golf swing.

- No matter how bad you are playing, it is always possible to play worse.

- The inevitable result of any golf lesson is the instant elimination of the one critical unconscious motion that allowed you to compensate for all of your many other errors.

- Everyone replaces his divot after a perfect approach shot.

---

1 Posted by "Fengibbon" at www.golfmagic.com

- A golf match is a test of your skill against your opponents' luck.

- It is surprisingly easy to hole a fifty foot putt. For a ten.

- Counting on your opponent to inform you when he breaks a rule is like expecting him to make fun of his own haircut.

- Nonchalant putts count the same as chalant putts.

- It's not a gimme if you're still five feet away.

- The shortest distance between any two points on a golf course is a straight line that passes directly through the center of a very large tree.

- You can hit a two-acre fairway 10 percent of the time and a two-inch branch 90 percent of the time.

- If you really want to get better at golf, go back and take it up at a much earlier age.

- Every time a golfer makes a birdie, he must subsequently make two triple bogeys to restore the fundamental equilibrium of the universe.

- If you want to hit a seven iron as far as Tiger Woods does, simply try to lay up just short of a water hazard.

- There are two things you can learn by stopping your backswing at the top and checking the position of your hands: how many hands you have, and which one is wearing the glove.

- A ball you can see in the rough from fifty yards away is not yours.

- If there is a ball on the fringe and a ball in the bunker, your ball is in the bunker. If both balls are in the bunker, yours is in the footprint

- A good drive on the eighteenth hole has stopped many a golfer from giving up the game.

- Golf is the perfect thing to do on a Sunday afternoon because you always end up having to pray a lot.

- If there's a storm rolling in, you'll be having the game of your life.

- Golf balls are like eggs. They're white. They're sold by the dozen. And you need to buy fresh ones each week.

♦ If your opponent has trouble remembering whether he shot a six or a seven, he probably shot an eight (or worse).

♦ A good golf partner is a nice guy who's always slightly worse than you are ... that's why I get so many calls to play with friends.

THE MEXICAN FISHERMAN (AUTHOR UNKNOWN)

The American investment banker was at the pier of a small coastal Mexican village when a small boat with just one fisherman docked.

Inside the small boat were several large yellow fin tuna. The American complimented the Mexican on the quality of his fish and asked how long it took to catch them.

"Only a little while," The Mexican replied.

The American then asked, "Why didn't you stay out longer and catch more fish?"

The Mexican said, "With this I have more than enough to support my family's needs."

The American then asked, "But what do you do with the rest of your time?"

The Mexican fisherman said, "I sleep late, fish a little, play with my children, take siesta with my wife, Maria, stroll into the village each evening where I sip wine and play guitar with my amigos, I have a full and busy life."

The American scoffed, "I am a Harvard MBA and I could help you. You should spend more time fishing, and with the proceeds, buy a bigger boat. With the proceeds from the bigger boat you could buy several boats. Eventually you would have a fleet of fishing boats. Instead of selling your catch to a middleman you would sell directly to the processor, eventually opening your own cannery. You would need to leave this small coastal fishing village and move to Mexico City, then Los Angeles, and eventually New York, where you would run your ever-expanding enterprise."

"But, how long will this all take?" the Mexican fisherman asked.

"Fifteen to twenty years," replied the American.

"But what then?" asked the Mexican.

The American laughed and said, "When the time is right you would announce an IPO and sell your company stock to the public and become very rich; you would make millions."

"Millions? . . . Then what?"

The American said, "Then you would retire. Move to a small coastal fishing village where you would sleep late, fish a little, play with your kids, take siesta with your wife, Maria, stroll to the village in the evenings where you could sip wine and play your guitar with your amigos."

The Philosophy of Ambiguity

When our daughter Julie was very young, I remember her asking me why sour cream had an expiration date. She also wondered out loud if there was another word for *synonym* and noted it was too bad the word *lisp* has an "s" in it. My wife, Bobbie, contends this tree didn't fall far from the nut. If you also love the philosophy of ambiguity, you'll enjoy these.

- If man evolved from monkeys and apes, why do we still have monkeys and apes?

- I went to a bookstore and asked the salesperson, "Where's the self-help section?" She said if she told me, it would defeat the purpose.

- What if there were no hypothetical questions?

- Where do forest rangers go to "get away from it all?"

- What do you do when you see an endangered animal eating an endangered plant?

- If a parsley farmer is sued, can they garnish his wages?

- Would a fly without wings be called a walk?

- Why do they lock gas station bathrooms? Are they afraid someone will clean them?

- Can vegetarians eat animal crackers?

- If the police arrest a mime, do they tell him he has the right to remain silent?

- Why do they put Braille on the drive-through bank machines?

- How do they get deer to cross the road only at those yellow road signs?

- What was the best thing before sliced bread?

- If you ate both pasta and antipasto, would you still be hungry?

- If you try to fail, and succeed, which have you done?

- Can an atheist get insurance against acts of God?

THINGS TO DO IN AN ELEVATOR

- When people get on, ask for their tickets.

- When there's only one other person in the elevator, tap them on the shoulder and then pretend it wasn't you.

- Ask if you can push the button for other people, but push the wrong ones.

- Hold the doors open and say you're waiting for your friend. After a while, let the doors close and say, "Hi Mike. How's your day been?"

- Drop a pen, wait until someone reaches to help pick it up, and say, "That's mine!"

- Push your floor button with your nose.

- Stand alone, and when the doors open tell people trying to get on that the car is full and that they should wait for the next one.

DEEP THOUGHTS

Here are some chin-stroking deep thoughts for you to ponder . . .

- I hope if dogs ever take over the world, and they choose a king, they don't just go by size, because I bet there are some Chihuahuas with some good ideas.

- When you go for a job interview, I think a good thing to ask is if they ever press charges.

- To me, boxing is like a ballet, except there's no music, no choreography, and the dancers hit each other.

BUMPER STICKER WISDOM

Over the years I have traveled to California many times. Of course, the freeways are legendary. You're either going eighty miles per hour in bumper to bumper traffic, or your crawling along at a snail's pace in bumper to bumper traffic. The only advantage of the latter over the former is you get a chance to read the bumper stickers. Here are a few favorites.

- Well, this day was a total waste of makeup.

- I started out with nothing and still have most of it left.

- If I throw a stick, will you leave?

- Who are these kids and why are they calling me Dad?

- Does your train of thought have a caboose?

- Adults are just kids who owe money.

- Can I trade this job for what's behind door number two?

- I'm still not sure if I understand ambiguity.

- The world is full of apathy, but I don't care.

- I always wanted to be a procrastinator.

- Is it time for your medication or mine?

- I'm not tense, just terribly, terribly alert.

- My karma ran over your dogma.

The Interview

Reaching the end of a job interview, the human resources person asked a young engineer fresh out of MIT what kind of salary he was looking for.

"Oh, something in the neighborhood of $140,000 a year, depending on the benefits package," he confidently replied.

"Well, what would you say to a package of five-week's vacation, fourteen paid holidays, full medical and dental, company matching retirement fund up to 50 percent of your salary, and a company car leased every two years, say a Mercedes or a Lexus?"

"Wow," are you kidding?" the young man exclaimed.

"Yeah, but you started it."

Westinghouse

A lady opened her refrigerator door and saw a rabbit sitting on one of the shelves.

"What are you doing in there?" she asked.

"This is a Westinghouse, isn't it?" he replied.

Why, yes," she answered.

"Well, I'm westing."

The Doorbell

A priest was walking down a residential street one day when he noticed a very small boy standing on a front porch, trying to reach a doorbell.

After watching the boy's failed efforts for some time, the priest crossed the street and walked up behind the little fellow. He placed his hand kindheartedly on the child's shoulder, leaned over and gave the doorbell a solid ring.

Crouching down to the boy's level, the priest smiled and asked, "And now what, my little man?"

"Now we run!"

A Few More Chin Strokers

♦ If Fed Ex and UPS were to merge, would they call it FedUps?

♦ Are Lipton Tea employees allowed to take coffee breaks?

♦ What hair color do they put on the driver's licenses of bald men?

♦ How much deeper would oceans be if sponges didn't live there?

♦ Why is the man who invests all your money called a broker?

♦ Why do croutons come in airtight packages? It's just stale bread to begin with.

♦ When cheese gets its picture taken, what does it say?

♦ Why are a wise man and a wise guy opposites?

♦ Why isn't 11 pronounced onety-one?

Authors Versus Editors

And, finally, since I'm an author, and editors are among my favorite people on the planet (yeah, right), here are some comments I could envision being written in the margins of manuscripts by one of them.

♦ Avoid clichés like the plague.

♦ Exaggeration is a billion times worse than understatement.

♦ If there's one thing I can't stand, it's intolerance.

♦ Prepositions are not words to end sentences with.

♦ One should never generalize.

"Happiness makes a person smile, but sadness can break a person's spirit"
(Proverbs 15:13).